PRAISE FOR *PRAYERS FOR THE GODDESS*

What a lovely string of pearls are the daily devotions in these elegant pages, waiting to caress the soul with beauty and insight! Prayers to the Goddess is a rare gift to all who sense Her presence and answer Her call. I look forward both to using the prayers and to gifting others with this new volume.

~ Holli S. Emore, M.Div. Executive Director
of Cherry Hill Seminary, author of *Pool of Lotus*

This book, its meditations and prayers, sing to my heart. Every initiate or priestess of the goddess should have this book by their bed, and maybe a copy on their altar, and one in the car to that as they travel along they can to see what the moon on the horizon on the road ahead is up to. I love this practice. Thank you for the simple beauty of it and its truth.

~ Normandi Ellis, *Dreams of Isis and Feasts of Light*

Prayers to the Goddess: A Moon Cycle Devotion sources our deep longings and brings into words compassion, nurturance, comfort, wisdom while helping us be mindful of our deep connection with the mystery, beauty and regenerative powers held in the grace and presence of Great Mother. Together in these pages we lift up our voices in the collective and remember our sense of awe in being alive as we connect to our grateful heart. If you are seeking connection you will find yourself opening this book many times over as the moon waxes and wanes.

~ Alisa Starkweather,
founder of the Red Tent Temple Movement

I thought this little book was glorious. I read it in one sitting, and it soothed me to read the prayers to the Goddess. The daily meditations and explanations were rich and valuable. It's a lovely devotional book.

~ Cristina Biaggi, *Activism into Art into Activism into Art:*
A Personal History of Feminist Art

The incantations in this wonderful book evoke a matriarchal time when prayers to the Goddess of the Cosmos were part of our daily world and calling on guidance from the Moon was second nature. There is no better way to begin and end a day than with a prayer that empowers, blesses and connects us to the teachings of our Mother Moon in all her phases. I plan to keep my copy on my night table.

~ Sudie Rakusin, *The Coloring Book for Big Girls*

Reading *Prayers to the Goddess: A Moon Cycle of Devotion* is like doing private ritual with your closest sisters. Anne and Genevieve guide us to invoke the Moon through her every cycle, honoring each phase with prayer. Then, turning deeper into the Mystery, we summon the Goddess within, inviting that deep intimacy into our hearts through beautiful prayers of personal devotions. This book is like walking through the dark night and having the moon appear from behind a cloud, lighting your way when you most need it. It will become a regular companion in your ritual.

~ Kathryn Ravenwood, *How to Create Sacred Water:*
A Guide to Rituals and Practices

What a sweet and instructive little prayer book, honoring—graphically—the phases of the Moon each month. A simple yet profound way to build awareness of the lunar cycles and our innate relationship to them, with affirmations and prayers to set a ceremonial tone.

~ Vicki Noble, co-creator of Motherpeace & author
of *Shakti Woman: Feeling Our Fire, Healing Our World*

This delightfully small book is an encouraging entrance and support for new language with which to converse and praise our Source of Being as Mother, as "She"; and gentle encouragement for making sacred space for self to commune with Her. We have lived in times starved for words and image of Her as sacred guide for our way, yet Moon has always been present. The devotional practice offered here includes simply seeking Her, looking for Her, which in itself is always rewarding; and enabling the remembering and invoking of Her indigenous trustworthy magic.

~ Glenys Livingstone Ph.D., *PaGaian Cosmology:
Re-inventing Earth-based Goddess Religion*

Enlightening, informative, inviting meditation, Prayers to the Goddess is a helpful resource. It is filled with daily moon cycle devotions that connect to She-Who-Is-Divine. Be blessed on your moon journey as you embrace this lovely guide.

~ Diann L. Neu, co-director of Women's Alliance
for Theology, Ethics, and Ritual (WATER)
and author of *Stirring WATERS: Feminist Liturgies for Justice*

Prayers to the Goddess clearly lays out an easy and accessible devotional schema nurturing personal and spiritual completeness in the divine language of the feminine, namely, that of the Great Mother. Employing the phases of the monthly lunar cycle, this concise book suggests daily prayers that may be quickly recited or used for full meditation—depending on the varying situations of its readers. The proposals offered may be for solitary use, shared with partners or in a group, employed as inspiration for writing or journal keeping, and as a form of 'bibliomancy' for providing guiding catalysts. Without doubt, many will enjoy and benefit from this well-designed and easy-to-use endeavour.

~ Professor Michael York, *Pagan Mysticism: Paganism as a World Religion*

Beautiful prayers to the Goddess to open your heart to the cycle of the Moon as you journey through a challenging era to greater consciousness and love for her presence in all creation.

~ Janine Canan, editor of *Love Is My Religion* by Mata Amritanandamayi

It has been a delight to sit with this book and find such a rich cornucopia of information and prayers! …The world needs to understand the power and beauty of prayers, and with this beautiful little book, it is an easy choice to pick up each day and lay down again at night. With a full year of daily prayers and information about the Moon's energy at any given time, I feel this book will be valued and treasured by many.

~ Anique Radiant Heart, High Priestess of the Australian Temple of the Global Goddess, creator of Goddess Inspired Music

This is a charming collection of prayers, meditations, affirmations and poetry designed to assist in opening the door to a deeper connection to the Feminine Divine as imaged by the eternal cycles of the moon. It is a rich source of inspiration for individuals and groups, for private meditation and for ritual. It channels the magic of the moon for inner development, awareness, harmony and healing in a month long journey of morning and evening devotions.

~ Candace C. Kant, Ph.D.,
Academic Dean, Cherry Hill Seminary

This book is a multifaceted invitation to illuminate the richness of the feminine spirit, and our relationship with it, so we gain strength for our unique expression in our families, our souls, and in the world. Succor for the soul, the prayers and poetry contained in this book elevate us to embrace the divine as a tool for healing, remembering and empowering ourselves daily.

~ Beth Wilson,
Meditations for New Mothers and The Recovering Feminist

I am frequently asked by women beginning their journey, "How do I practice?" This book would be a great resource for women asking this question and for those who want to add more depth to their work. As we continue to expand what it means to have a practice as Goddess women, this book can provide insight and direction.

~ Jade River, *In Our Bones*

A beautiful book! The descriptions of the Moon in each of her phases help us pay better attention, and then the prayers guide us into deeper communion with Her.

~ Charlene Spretnak, *Lost Goddesses of Early Greece*

What a treasure this book is! So designed to be doable in our busy world and yet so poignant and meaningful. These devotions have nurtured my heart and soothed my soul. Their tender messages have touched me and fortified me to open my heart and be the light in the world that honors Her. The prayers in this book captures the love that She offers and sends us forth to be more of who we thought we could be. We sorely need that love in our lives and in the world.

~ Delphine DeMore, Ph.D., High Priestess and co-founder of Goddess Spirit Rising

PRAYERS TO THE
GODDESS

A MOON CYCLE DEVOTION

BY GENEVIEVE CHAVEZ MITCHELL
AND ANNE KEY

Printed in the United States of America
ISBN: 978-0-9969617-6-9

Published by: Goddess Ink
www.goddess-ink.com

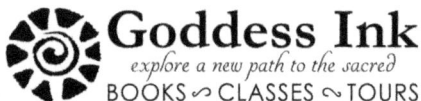

Goddess Ink
explore a new path to the sacred
BOOKS ∽ CLASSES ∽ TOURS

Cover & Interior design by Rebekkah Dreskin
www.blameitonrebekkah.com

Illustrations by Fifi Lug
www.etsy.com/shop/mydailyillustration

All rights reserved, used with permission.

CONTENTS

ABOUT THIS BOOK

T his book is a daily devotional to help you connect with the Divine. We envision the Divine in Her feminine aspect, and we offer these daily prayers as a way to interweave your life with the Divine. This is a guidebook that speaks the language of Great Mother: acknowledging your precious life, inviting your deeper awareness, and celebrating your immense capacity for joy.

The daily devotions begin with the Dark Moon. For ideas on how to use this book and hints on following the daily practice, see "Ways to Experience this Journey."

Many blessings as you begin your journey.

~ Genevieve & Anne
  Albuquerque, New Mexico
  The Land of Enchantment

WAYS TO EXPERIENCE THIS JOURNEY

How To Keep Track of Days

You might consider beginning this journey by looking at a calendar and determining the first day of the lunar cycle. Then, align the days in the guide book with your calendar. Marking your own calendar will establish your experience with this lunar guide, bringing your spiritual practice into your daily life.

This journey begins on the Dark Moon (when no Moon is visible—marked on your calendar by a black circle). The New Moon is the first sliver of light that the Moon shows. The entire lunar cycle is 29.531 days, which means that it doesn't fit perfectly into a conventional calendar. But, that's what makes our attention even more powerful!

Missed a day? Remember—this is a non-judgment zone. If you get busy and forget a day or two, just pick up on the day's reading and move on. No worries!

And, if following the Moon cycle is confusing, you can simply use the book for a month as a daily reading. Don't worry about the Moon's phase; just enjoy the prayers.

Daily Practice

For some of us, reading the daily prayer—quickly before the day begins and then at night just before we dive deep into the short time we have for sleep—will be enough. For others, a quieter, meditative time might be in order, perhaps journaling or writing your own prayers.

Whatever your situation, consider trying to find a quiet place to do your practice. Read the title of the day's prayer, then take a breath. Close your eyes and let the title settle. Then open, and read the prayer. Give yourself 5 full breaths afterwards to sit with the message. After, acknowledge yourself, grateful you found the time for this renewal and connection, for this time will help you be your most grace-filled, loving, and genuine self. In the evening, take time to breathe, open to the evening prayer, and allow yourself to connect with your soul.

For Those Able to View the Sky

If you are lucky enough to have a view of the sky (and even better if you have a view of the horizon), try reading the morning prayer at Sunrise and the evening prayer after dusk. Experiencing the light of the morning and the deep darkness of night will bring you to a closer relationship with the journeys of the celestial bodies and your relationship with the cycles of the Earth, and this will facilitate your own deeper embodiment. You will begin to find that you are not living "on" Earth and viewing the cosmos from afar, but that you are a living part of the Earth and the cosmos. Which, of course, you are!

We have added suggestions for how to see the Moon. Give them a try and see if you can find Her during the day as well. Please check online to find the moonrise and moonset times in your own time zone, and then determine the best time for you to see Her.

Southern and Northern Hemisphere Orientations

The Moon is oriented differently in the Southern and Northern hemispheres. For observers in the Southern Hemisphere, the Waxing Moon is a "C" shape. In the Northern Hemisphere, the Waxing Moon is a backward "C." At the equator, the Waxing Moon appears more like a "U."

Conversely, observers in the Southern Hemisphere will see the Waning Moon as a backward "C," and those in the Northern Hemisphere will see the Waning Moon as a "C."

So, while the entire Earth experiences the same Moon phase, we see the shape of the Waxing and Waning Moons differently.

This book is written and published in Albuquerque, New Mexico. The drawings of the Moon in this book show the phases as they appear in the Northern Hemisphere, where our spiritual practice is grounded. In the descriptions of the Moon phases, we have mentioned that the crescent will appear differently depending on where the observer lives.

Bedside Altar

This book may become your bedside companion—the one you look to first thing in the morning and the last thing in the evening. If you have room on your bedside table, consider putting a beautiful cloth to lay the book upon, thus creating a bit of sacred space.

Other Ways to Use this Book

- Share the prayers with your partner at the beginning and end of each day for the Moon cycle
- Gather with a group and use the prayers to open and close ritual
- Use the prayers as a prompt for journal writing
- Use the book for "bibliomancy:" close your eyes, and open the book to the page you are guided towards, and read the poem for that day

BEGINNING THE JOURNEY
A Day of Preparation

───── ⌒ஃ⌒ ─────

As you prepare to embark on this Moon cycle, take a moment today to prepare. Along with this short morning and evening ritual, do whatever you can to clear the space for this journey.

Consider taking a ritual bath, or set aside time to create an altar with your intentions. If you have just a minute or two, try burning some incense or sage to smudge. If possible, finish an outstanding task. Do what you can to clear the space—outside and inside—to begin this Moon cycle.

Morning Ritual

Take a few moments this morning of the Dark Moon. Light a candle and say these words:

Holy Flame
Ignite the fire within me.
May my heart-fire shine through the day.

Stay focused on the candle flame for a few moments, then close your eyes. Sit for a moment. Then snuff the flame, but carry its light within you throughout the day.

Evening Ritual

Take a few moments this evening of the Dark Moon. Light a candle and say these words:

Holy Flame
Cradle the fire within me.
May my heart-fire glow through the night.

Stay focused on the candle flame for a few moments, then close your eyes. Sit for a moment, then snuff the flame, but carry its light within you throughout the night.

WAXING MOON CYCLE

WANING MOON CYCLE

1

DARK MOON

The Dark Moon rises as the Sun rises, and it sets as the Sun sets, so the Moon and Sun are in direct alignment. The Moon is in the shadow of the Sun's glare, so it is completely obscured. The Dark Moon is the first Moon phase.

Intriguing, isn't it, that at the moment the Moon is dark, the side of the Moon we never see (the Dark Side of the Moon!) is fully illuminated. Consider the Dark Moon as a time to welcome into your awareness of parts of you that you don't "see" or that you don't show others. It is a time to embrace your full self, opening to the complexity of being a human being,with the complete range of emotions—from the muck and mire of our angry, ungenerous aspects to the pure flowering of our love and compassion. All this we can know in the forgiving darkness.

This may seem hard now, but at the end of this Moon cycle, it will be easier. Take a moment to journal how you are feeling at this Dark Moon. Be honest, allowing the healing light of the Sun to touch all of the places within that are on the Dark Side of your Moon.

HELD IN YOUR ARMS

Great Goddess
I see myself
Held in Your arms.
I see my family and friends
Held in Your arms.
I see my neighbors
Held in Your arms.
I see my city
Held in Your arms.
I see my state
Held in Your arms.
I see my country
Held in Your arms.
I see this hemisphere
Held in Your arms.
I see the world
Held in Your arms.
Everyone, everything, always,
Great Goddess, in Your arms.

DARKNESS

I seek the comfort of the night
But all I find are the thoughts of the day
Haunting my soul.

Dear Goddess,
Find me in the vast stretch of humanity
Reach your hand to mine
Envelop me in your arms
That the darkness may touch my dark places
That the darkness may nourish me
That the darkness may restore me.

Hear my call, dear Goddess,
and keep me through the night.
Let your love overpower my thoughts
Let your love infuse my dreams
Let your love hold me until the break of dawn.

2

NEW MOON

TThe New Moon appears as a faint thread of light. From the Northern Hemisphere, the light appears on the right side of the moon. You may be able to see Her in the evening, low in the western sky. This is a wonderful time to set an intention and focus on nurturing your spirit.

Pay attention to the subtle messages that you receive from your environment. Listen for the unspoken communication of your friends and lovers, open to the delicate blessings of a kind word, a simple gesture. Know that the light of this New Moon is a signal of hope and love. Even if you can't see Her, remember that She is there. Embrace Her as a sign that you are ready to move forward.

BREATHE ME

Breathe me, Breath of She Who Loves,
that I may love what You love.

Breathe me, Breath of She Who Gives,
that I may give as You give.

Breathe me, Breath of She Who Comforts,
that I may comfort Your own.

Breathe me, Breath of She Who Creates,
that I may create Your world.

Breathe me, Breath of She Who Births,
that I may birth a world of grace.

Breathe me, Breath of She Who Brings Peace,
that I may be peace.

Breathe me, Breath of She Who Loves,
that I may love what You love.

KEEPER OF MY SOUL

As I enter this cave of darkness

I dwell in Her, Keeper of my soul.

I meet with the Ancient One
who knows my innermost being.

She breathes my breath and gives me life.

She lights the night with her Essence.

She protects me with Her Divine Grace.

She dwells in me,

I dwell in Her, Keeper of my soul.

3

YOUNG WAXING CRESCENT MOON

The Young Crescent Moon, with her tiny arc of light, rises in the daytime before noon and becomes visible in the day sky. Look for Her in the eastern sky in the afternoon, or try and catch Her in the western sky just after sunset.

In the winter in the Northern Hemisphere, the Young Crescent Moon may look like a "U." This shape mirrors the horns of a cow. As a giver of life, in the form of milk, cows have been revered throughout time as a symbol of woman's ability to nurture. You may remember in Marion Zimmer Bradley's book *Mists of Avalon* that the priestesses had a Crescent Moon tattooed on their foreheads.

The Young Waxing Crescent Moon brings the energy to ask: What is it you want to birth, to nurture, to lovingly bring to fruition? A task? A relationship? An exploration? Do you have something particular you want to manifest in this moon cycle? You may wish to follow this guide through the entire cycle, or you may wish to allow for further guides and illuminations, honoring your flexibility.

Leave yourself open tonight to hear the whisperings of the Stars and the gentle illumination of the Moon.

THE GREATEST GOOD

Nourish me Gracious Goddess:

Fill me

So that my tongue will only speak what is needed

So that my heart remains open to You

So that my thoughts will delight in You

So that I will have the grace

>   to know my shortcomings and correct them

>   to know when to speak and when to be silent

>   to know wisdom in my actions and kindness in my exchanges

>   to recognize a moment of service

>   for the greatest good.

CRESCENT MOON

The Sun has set and the sky darkens

I surrender to the deep velvet of night once again.

As I turn my face toward the heavens

I see Your Crescent Moon,

A shining beacon,

I did not realize I was holding my breath;

I breathe You, and everything releases.

I am filled with hope,

My soul rejoices,

My heart sings,

And I know that the way is prepared.

4

WAXING CRESCENT MOON

The Waxing Crescent Moon is a distinct shape. In the Northern Hemisphere, the shape is a backwards "C"; in the Southern Hemisphere, the shape is a regular "C"; and at the equator, the shape is more of a "U."

You may be looking at a situation in your life that needs your steady attention, at some encounter or chore that you have been avoiding, at some gift you want to give but have hesitated to offer. This is a great time to pour your intention into action. It may take courage, it may require persistent effort, but you are ready to take full responsibility for shaping your direction.

Consider spending a moment at your altar tonight. Is there something you need to add? If your vision is unclear, know that as the light of the Moon increases, so will your clarity.

GODDESS OF ALL NATURE

With morning Sun, we are blessed

With the beauty of the blossom, we are blessed

With the majesty of the mountain, we are blessed

With tempest, gale, and the evening breeze,
we are blessed

With the cloudburst and the rainbow, we are
blessed

With beings who fly, who swim, who burrow and
who walk our Earth, we are blessed

With the rocks and the trees, we are blessed

With the waters of the Earth, we are blessed

With the power of the ocean, we are blessed

With the beauty of all of nature, known and
unknown, we are blessed

With She who dwells in all, we are blessed

Always, we are blessed.

GREAT AND LIVING GODDESS

Confident in Your protection,
I fly to Your light.

I invoke Your power and majesty,
I long for Your healing touch.

I call on You;
hold my hand, calm my trembling heart,
restore me.

Hear me Great and Living Goddess.
Blessed are You.

5

WAXING CRESCENT MOON

A Waxing Moon grows each day as more of the Moon is illuminated. This increase of light brings about an increase in attention to the outside world. The Waxing Crescent Moon rises before noon and becomes visible in the daytime sky. It grows more visible around sunset and sets before midnight. Look to the western sky in the evening to find Her.

As She increases, do you feel yourself filling with Her light? This is a time to enjoy beginnings and the excitement of early efforts and awareness, to truly celebrate your participation in the great cycle of life-energy as expressed in the Moon.

Open yourself to Her illumination, and know that you are held.

TENDER GROWTH

This morning I am a new green shoot,

Head pushing through the crust of the Earth.

Birthed into this new day

Feeling the gentle drops of dew

Sensing the warm rays of the Sun

I am tender and new,
held in the loving hands of the Goddess.

Fearless,

I burst forth.

I AM GRATEFUL

I am grateful, to be here, alive with my life, my one,
unique, uncommon, very common life.

I am grateful for the interesting, challenging,
beautiful, imperfect situations, conditions,
and people in my life.

I am grateful for Your gifts;
they are precious, lovely, and generous.

Remind me, Holy One,
that You are my Reason, my Yes, my Life.

I am blessed. I am grateful.

6

LATE WAXING CRESCENT MOON

This is the sixth day since the Dark Moon. The last day of this phase brings us to the Late Waxing Crescent. The light of the Moon increases and the crescent thickens; tomorrow is the First Quarter Moon.

What is growing within you? What is increasing? What is illuminating? Where do you need to push, and where do you need to surrender? Do you need to be still and allow the Moon's light to nourish you? Or do you need to get up and move forward? Be kind and firm with yourself, taking what you need, letting go of old perspectives and opinions. Be aware of the actual unfolding of your thoughts and emotions and how these may evolve with your newfound confidence.

BEAUTY

Great Mother
Open my eyes to the beauty before me.

Great Mother
Open my eyes to the beauty behind me.

Great Mother
Open my eyes to the beauty above me.

Great Mother
Open my eyes to the beauty below me.

Great Mother
Open my eyes to the beauty within me.

Great Mother
Open my eyes to the beauty around me.

SURRENDER TO THANKS

Before I surrender to the nurturing arms of sleep,

I give thanks for the beauty of this day.

For the beauty of this existence

For the beauty of the natural world

For the beauty of the Stars and the Moon

I give thanks for love of this day.

For the love that I have found

For the love that I have given

For the love that surrounds me

I give thanks

and surrender to the nurturing arms of sleep.

7

EARLY FIRST QUARTER MOON

The first quarter Moon occurs at the moment the Moon has completed a fourth of its orbit around Earth, hence the name. It is also called Half Moon as we can see exactly 50% of the Moon's surface illuminated.

You can find Her overhead in the evening sky. Even just half-lit, She is bright! Consider that a lesson, reminding you that your periods of struggle or fatigue or sadness are just part of your precious life, to be cherished and learned from. Even in the moments when you don't feel fully there, or completely in your power—you still shine bright.

LET THE WAY BE OPEN

Sing through my voice
Play through my hands
Let the way be open.

Sing through my voice
Play through my hands
Let the way be open.

Sing through my voice
Play through my hands
Let the way be open.

GREAT GODDESS

Great Goddess,
be in our mind and in our thinking

Great Goddess,
be in our hearts and in our perceiving

Great Goddess,
be in our mouth and in in our speaking

Great Goddess,
be in our hands and in our working

Great Goddess,
be in our feet and in our walking

Great Goddess,
be in our bodies and in our loving

Great Goddess,
be with us all the days of our lives and beyond

Great Goddess,
be with us now.

8

FIRST QUARTER MOON

The First Quarter Moon rises near the middle of the day and sets around the middle of the night in most areas. Look for Her overhead in the afternoon and in the western sky in the evening. The First Quarter is the second Moon phase.

Spend a moment in Her light tonight, letting Her Moonbeams nurture you. Allow Her light to illuminate what you are manifesting.

Or, just spend a moment giving yourself the space to open and be nourished. You cannot pour from an empty cup; allow the energy of the waxing cycle to fill you, replenish you, and rejuvenate you.

MORNING BRIGHT

Morning glory, sunlit sky,
flight of swallows, fill my eyes

Wonder prevails, awake my soul,
spark of Goddess, the reason I rise

Let all I am or say or do reveal in me
Your beautiful light

Sunrise glory, light and joy,
Goddess of all, morning bright.

PRAYER TO THE WAXING FIRST QUARTER
WHEN SHE IS HALF FULL

I find You low in the western sky,
bright white Goddess,

Even half-lit,
Your beacon gleams.

Light my path to fullness

Light my path to wholeness

Light my path to all that is holy

Oh Goddess, beacon for my soul.

9

LATE FIRST QUARTER

This last day of the First Quarter Moon reminds us that we are halfway through the waxing cycle, on our way to the Full Moon. Find Her shining bright in the western sky this evening.

With this reminder, keep in mind what you are manifesting, or what you are bringing forth. Is there something you need to do now to keep things "on track?" If so, spend a little time in Her light tonight, gaining strength, energy, wisdom, and whatever else you need to move forward. Let Her light be the wind under your wings.

WEAVER

Weaving, Weaver, spin me into strong yarn, and
weave me into exquisite, magnificent patterns.

Weave my dreaming

Weave my birthings

Weave my treasures

Weave my stories

Weave my ancestors

Weave Your Mystery

Weave Your Strength

Weave Your Song

Weave Your Wisdom

Weave Your Light into the tapestry of my life.

LONGING

Goddess Spirit Divine,
Longing for You

> To envelop me
>
> To hold me
>
> To unfold me
>
> To find rest and quiet and stillness
>
> To be alone with You,
>
> To find myself in You

Longing to
Surrender to and be surrounded by You,
Goddess Spirit Divine.

10

YOUNG WAXING GIBBOUS MOON

The Young Waxing Gibbous Moon is the next major lunar phase. "Waxing" means that the Moon's light is growing brighter. "Gibbous" refers to the shape of the illuminated portion of the Moon, which is larger than the half-circle shape at First Quarter but smaller than a full circle. The word "gibbous" comes from the Latin for "hump" or "bulge." We love the idea that the Moon is indeed bulging—pregnant, one might say—with the power of manifestation. From this point on, the Moon grows brighter and brighter. Find Her in the evening in the eastern sky.

Feel the creative energy growing inside you; the increasing fullness awakens novel ideas and births fresh perspectives. Allow Her light to shine new brilliance on your long-pursued projects and dreams. Spend some time in Her generative light, nourishing yourself and your manifestation.

HEART BLOSSOM

Day unfolds, petal by petal

As light spreads across the horizon.

My heart unfolds, petal by petal

Flowering, welcoming dawn's delight.

I am a blossom of the Goddess

Full of color, scent, and life

The love of the Goddess blossoms in my soul.

EVENING BENEDICTION

Bless me O Goddess, as night descends

Bless me O Goddess, as stars arise

Bless me O Goddess, be my protection

Bless me O Goddess, rest my tired body and soul

Bless me O Goddess, shelter those I love

Bless me O Goddess, guide my dreams

Bless me O Goddess, let me know Your peace

Bless me O Goddess, grant me wisdom

Bless me O Goddess,
I am Yours, in my sleeping and in my waking

Bless me O Goddess.

11

WAXING GIBBOUS MOON

The Waxing Gibbous Moon rises in mid-afternoon and sets early in the morning. She is so bright! Can you feel Her? These days of increase can be energizing. Look for Her this evening in the eastern sky or overhead.

She is moving closer to full illumination. What flower buds are close to opening within you? Can you feel the readiness and gentle urgency of your own process? What petals are beginning to unfurl? What will blossom with the Full Moon?

As every night brings us closer to the Full Moon, spend some time with Her. Let Her light nurture your bud, and feel the corners of your mouth turn up into a smile as you bask in the pleasure of the coming blossoming of the Full Moon.

TEMPLE OF THE GODDESS

I am a Temple of the Goddess

I am made in Her image

I am filled with Her radiant beauty

I manifest Her vibrant splendor

I radiate Her luminous body in my being

I am Her shining beacon of light

I am a Temple of the Goddess

She and I are One.

WE CALL YOUR NAME

We call Your name,
Flame of Truth
We call Your name,
Great Mother
We call Your name,
Breath of Life
We call Your name,
Mighty One
We call Your name,
She Who Gives
We call Your name,
She Who Takes Away
We call Your name,
Wellspring of Compassion
We call Your name,
Beloved.

Open us to insight, grace,
discernment, and illumination
Guide us to Your Light, Your Wisdom
Guide us to You.

12

WAXING GIBBOUS MOON

As She moves toward full, She is bright in the sky. Find Her in the eastern sky this evening, and spend a moment bathing in Her light.

This is a moment to know yourself. Do you need to push a little harder? Do you need to let go and surrender to the process? Do you need to put yourself out there and shine brighter? Do you need to take in all the light to gather the strength to move forward?

Hold yourself in the strong hands of compassion and find your way into the beginnings of wisdom. A deepened, more subtle awareness may come. Listen to this expanded, utterly gentle voice that is your deepest self, and let it guide you.

WELCOMING THE DAY WITH JOY

All wondrous Goddess

The Sun rises shining across these lands
wrought by Your very hands.

The cool air of morning is a balm to the Earth,
just as Your love is to every soul.

The birds welcome the day with song,
and my heart is filled with joy.

I close my eyes
And keep this moment
For all of my days on Earth.

HELD IN GENTLE MOONLIGHT

Your gentle light shines from above
Softening the edges

    Blurring what I thought was fixed
    Relaxing what I thought was rigid
    Yielding what I thought was unyielding
    Opening what I thought was closed.

Dear Goddess, envelop me in Your gentle light.

13

LATE WAXING GIBBOUS MOON

In the days prior to the full Moon, the nights are bright and beautiful. She glows in the night sky, bathing everything in Her soft light.

The Moon reflects the Sun's light, so in these days we can feel the invigorating light of the Sun for almost 24 hours. How does the Moon reflect the coming-to-fruition in yourself? Can you feel the infinite space of possibility that invites and enfolds you? What is being energized? What photosynthesis is taking place? What flower is on the verge of bursting into blossom?

Illuminate your outward path of projects and responsibilities, giving support to lovers and friends, standing up courageously for what you believe, tending to children and to all beings in need, participating joyfully in the dance of life.

MORNING BLESSINGS
FROM THE GREAT MOTHER

The Sun rises
Blessings from the Great Mother

Bird song fills the air
Blessings from the Great Mother

Petals unfurl
Blessings from the Great Mother

Gentle wind ruffles my hair
Blessings from the Great Mother

My heart opens to the day
Blessings from the Great Mother

NIGHT BLESSINGS
FROM THE GREAT MOTHER

Sky deepens
Blessings from the Great Mother

Everything stills
Blessings from the Great Mother

The body relinquishes the day
Blessings from the Great Mother

Cares fall away
Blessings from the Great Mother

Dreams await
Blessings from the Great Mother

14

ALMOST FULL MOON

The Moon rises in late afternoon and sets very early in the morning, so you have a chance to bathe in Her glory even before She is completely full. The light and energy of the Moon can heighten your emotions, feelings, and dreams. This is a wonderful time to do a Moon bath. Sit in a spot—inside or outside—where you are covered in the soft light of the Moon. If possible, try this "sky clad" (without clothes!).

Close your eyes and let Her light awaken every cell within you. If you are manifesting something, imagine it held in your hands, and lift it up to Her light. If you are writing, put your pages under her Moonbeams. If you are healing, open your heart and soul to Her restorative gaze.

ILLUMINE ME

As Your light brings life to this day,
Illumine me

As the dawn breaks
Awaken my heart with joy

As the refreshing dew waters the Earth
Water my soul with Your Grace.

As the Sun warms my face
The edges of my lips curve upward
And I smile.

GOODNIGHT BELOVED ONE

Goodnight Beloved One
I thank You for Your blessing.
Goodnight Beloved One
I thank You for this day.
In Your full glory I will stand in awe
At dawn on the morrow.

Now, held in Your sweet, dark embrace,
I say
Goodnight Beloved One
I thank You for Your blessing
Goodnight Beloved One
I thank You for this day.

15
FULL MOON

The Full Moon appears in the night sky when the Sun and the Moon are aligned on opposite sides of the Earth. She shines brightly all night long. Astronomically speaking, a Full Moon occurs at the exact moment when the Moon and the Sun are on opposite sides of the Earth. The reason this instant is so short is that all three bodies are in constant motion.

Experience this moment as you are held between the two most prominent celestial bodies. Enjoy your "moment in the Sun" (remember, the Moon reflects the Sun's light!). Let the soft light of the Moon blur all of the sharp edges, and sink into bliss. Consider preparing a special cup of tea or pouring a sweet libation. If you have a partner, this is a wonderful time to share a sacred moment.

No matter how you enter into the space, give yourself just a little time tonight to nourish yourself and all that you bring forth.

GLORIOUS

Glorious Sun, light of all eternity
Light from endless light proceeding
Let Your beams upon us shine.

The soft refreshing dew
Falls upon the drooping flower
So our fainting hearts renew
By Your love's restoring power.

Let the glow of Your pure love
All fears and doubt disperse
In the radiance from above
Our hearts are full to burst.

Oh Glorious Sun of grace
May Your light be ever in our hearts
Shine upon our way to guide us
That from our path we will not part.

MAMA LUNA

Mama Luna, lamp of our night

Shine Your blessings on us tonight.

Mama Luna, source of healing

Spirit and grace, light revealing,

Mama Luna, waxing, waning

Full and new, ever changing.

Mama Luna, shining bright

Lead us to You, show us Your light.

16

FULL MOON

Under the sweet light of the Full Moon, spend a moment just "soaking it in." Invite yourself to celebrate the joyous satisfaction of full-fill-ment. This sphere in the sky is now as totally revealed and illuminated as it can be; let it symbolize your dreams and hopes ultimately realized. Imagine your beautiful self-recognized by all and profoundly loved by yourself.

Let the glowing orb of this Full Moon connect you to the numberless generations of beings who came before you on the planet Earth and feel the rightness of your presence here. You belong. You and the Moon are one.

RADIANT HEART

Radiant Heart, send a spark
To light the fire in my heart this morning.

May I be Your hands, Your voice, Your heart here
On this earthly plane.
May I serve to:

Wash what is soiled

Water what is dry

Heal what is wounded

Bend what is rigid

Warm what is cold

And find what is lost

All in the name of Divine Love
From Your radiant heart.

GREAT MOTHER OF THE COSMOS

Great Mother of the Cosmos
Guardian of the Galaxies
Giver of Life,
The very stars sparkle
Honoring the Great Mother.
The Moon beams
Honoring the Great Mother.
The comet flashes
Honoring the Great Mother.
The sky sings
Honoring the Great Mother.

17

FULL MOON

TThe Moon continues to appear full, lighting up the sky but rising later each night. This is the apex, the climax, of our journey outward. The Moon will begin waning tomorrow, our signal to start our journey inward.

On this last night of full illumination, bask in the energy and rejuvenation of the Moon's light. If there is anything you'd like to finish before embarking on the journey inward, now is the time. Let Her radiance fill you, lift you up; the energy of the cosmos supports you.

GIVER OF LIFE

Giver of Life

You give us all we need, You provide, protect,
and surround us with radiant blessings.

We are filled with gratitude.

You give us the abundant drops of rain,
the plentiful crops, and the cycles of seasons.
We thank You.

You give us the mountains,
the valleys the rivers, the oceans,
creatures of the air, the water, and the land.
We thank You.

You give us the Moon, the Stars,
and the galaxies without number.
We thank You.

You give us this breath of life,
this fire of spirit, this body to serve You.
We thank You.

Thank You O Giver of life.

EMBRACE OF NIGHT

I feel every moment of the day

In my muscles, in my bones, on my skin.

Before I enter the sweetness
Of the embrace of night

I breathe out the day

    I unwind my limbs

    I relinquish my thoughts

    I surrender my heart

And I enter the embrace of night,

Open, prepared, and yearning

For Your healing.

18

EARLY WANING GIBBOUS MOON

The Moon begins Her next phase, the Waning Gibbous. See Her either late at night or early in the morning; She will rise just a couple of hours after sunset.

The Waning Gibbous sets us on the path inward. When you begin this path, you bring all of the love, energy, and radiance of the Full Moon with you. Shine this healing light far down your inward path. What do you find there that is in need of healing? What tangles can be unwound? What old hurts beg for the balm of kindness? Allow the light to touch your deepest, most tender wounds, bringing love and nourishment to each step.

Surrender to the cycle of moving out and moving in, knowing that attention to each is necessary to live our lives fully.

SEARCH ME

Search me O Goddess

Search me O Goddess,
know my heart

Search me O Goddess,
direct my thoughts

Search me O Goddess,
cleanse and purify me

Search me O Goddess,
strengthen me

Search me O Goddess,
guide me to You

Search me O Goddess,
impart Your wisdom

Search me O Goddess,
let me be always found in You.

I SURRENDER

My footsteps still, my body in repose,
I surrender.

My eyes grow dim, my mind quiets,
I surrender.

My breath slows, my voice goes silent,
I surrender.

My troubles are absent, my spirit safe,
I surrender.

My trust is steadfast, my devotion complete,
I surrender.

Bathed in Your evening Splendor,
I surrender.

My soul returns to the Great Womb of Darkness,
and *I surrender.*

19

WANING GIBBOUS MOON

As the Moon wanes, She rises later every night. Find her later in the evening in the eastern sky; in the morning, look overhead or in the western sky. Check and see what Her rise and set time is for you. Try and watch Her rise in the eastern sky.

During these first days of the Waning Moon, take a minute to think about adding something to your altar that symbolizes your turn inward. On this journey, is there something you want to find as your look deep within yourself? Is there something within that you want to bolster? Revisit that inner wound that seeks healing.

PRAYER FOR OTHERS

In the quiet of this morning light, I pray for others.

I ask blessings on those I love and those who I don't love, those within and outside my circle.

I ask blessings on those, like me, who are wounded and flawed.

I ask blessings on those who tend my city, state, and nation, bless them with wisdom and kindness.

I ask blessings on our worldwide family, may we recognize our connection.

I ask blessings on the creatures of the Earth, the winged ones, those that live in the water and under the Earth, for they too are my kin.

This day, may I release my judgments and fears.

May I be a spirit of love and grace in the world today.

THIS PATH

This path to the Center

This path to the Origin

This path to Your Creation—

Illuminate this path and

Open the gates to this Mystery.

Open the way to Your Center.

Give me the heart and the strength
to follow this path

Celebrating this journey to You.

20

WANING GIBBOUS MOON

Still so bright in the sky, the Moon dims a little every day. As She rises later in the evening, She begins to set later in the morning. Find her in the morning overhead or in the western sky.

As She darkens a little each day, move a little deeper inside yourself. What do you find? What are you illuminating in the deep, rich darkness within? What are you holding tenderly? What needs the nourishing light of the Moon? Let yourself relax as you inquire, allowing your awareness to notice the small, subtle changes that may be taking place. Sometimes we have to catch up to ourselves, to see, "Oh, that's right, I no longer believe that old story—I've begun to know the fuller truth, the more holistic view of myself." This may be a time to sweep out the debris of already outmoded ideas, to acknowledge that, yes, I have really changed; I really can act differently, live differently.

Let yourself be held in Her strong hands of compassion as you journey inward.

THIS IS MY MOTHER'S WORLD

This is my Mother's world, and to my listening ears

All nature sings, and round me rings,
the music of the spheres.

This is my Mother's world,
I rest me in the thought

Of rocks and trees, of skies and seas—
Her hands the wonders wrought.

This is my Mother's world,
the birds their carols raise

The morning light, the lily white,
declare their Maker's praise.

This is my Mother's world,
She shines in all that's fair

In the rustling grass, I hear Her pass,
She speaks to me everywhere.

LADY OF THE DARK

Lady of the dark

Empty me of the day

Fill me with Your Presence

Guard me

Hold me

Touch me

Free me

Transform me.

Lady of the Dark

I open to receive Your love

From Your body to mine

From Your heart to mine

Lady of the Dark.

21

WANING GIBBOUS MOON

As the waning cycle continues, the Moon rises later and later in the evening. Unless you are a night owl (!), these are your last moments to see Her at night. Check for Her rise and set times, and take a moment to bathe in her soft light.

As Her light dims each day, journey deeper inside. This may take courage and tolerance, as you may find material that challenges your view of yourself. Remember that you contain the full range of human possibility—you have done some awful things in your life, and you have done sublimely good, generous things in your life. As you explore, see if you can embrace the full range of your personality, meeting it with unconditional love.

THANKS TO THE GIVER OF LIFE

Thanks to You O Giver of Life.
Thanks for all that I receive.

Thanks for grace that I cannot measure,
for flowers, sky, and tree.

Thanks for prayers that You have answered,
and for those that You have not.

Thanks for storms that I have I weathered,
thanks for grace that I have sought.

Thanks for joy and hope and comfort,
thanks for peace that You provide.

Thanks to You, O Giver of Life,
for staying always at my side.

I BREATHE IN THE DIVINE

A moment of silence at day's end
I Breathe in the Divine.

Finding the Earth under my feet
I Breathe in the Divine.

Stretching to the stars above my head
I Breathe in the Divine.

Falling deep into my soul
I Breathe in the Divine.

Surrendering to Her arms
I Breathe in the Divine.

22

LATE WANING GIBBOUS MOON

In these last days of the Waning Gibbous Moon, look for the Moon in the morning overhead or in the western sky. As light decreases each day, so do our ties with the outward world. We steadily look inward, feeling the pull of our deep subconscious.

Take a moment at your altar. Remember the piece you added to represent your journey? Pick it up and look at it. Does it provide you with new inklings of the nature of your quest? You may find that your altar not only strengthens you as you move forward but also shows you tiny flashes of inspiration, like starbursts, that appear in the darkness. Ask yourself where this path is taking you.

Know that you are held in the vast welcoming arms of the Divine.

TODAY

Yesterday is but a dream
Make every yesterday a dream of happiness.

Tomorrow is only a vision
Make every tomorrow a vision of hope

But today—today is the moment to live.

May every breath I take, dear Goddess,
be drawn with purpose.

I SEARCH FOR YOU, GREAT GODDESS

Hectic day stills to night
I search for You, Great Goddess

Darkness washes over twilight
I search for You, Great Goddess

Toil finally comes to an end
I search for You, Great Goddess

The path to dream I do wend
I search for You, Great Goddess

As I cross the veil to sleep
I search for You, Great Goddess.

I surrender to the deep,
And I search for You, Great Goddess.

23

EARLY LAST QUARTER MOON

As She rises later and later, find Her in the morning in the eastern sky or maybe even high overhead. Know that She is with us, day and night—visible and invisible. This is the third Moon phase: the Last Quarter. She has moved another fourth of the way around Earth, to the third quarter position.

These are powerful days to consider how you bring the light (consciousness) to your dark (unconscious) self. What do you need to see with your clearest, most compassionate gaze? What do you need to know, feeling the truth of it deep in yourself? What do you need to know that you don't even know you need to know? What is the landscape of the dark side of your Moon?

These moments in the Waning Moon are excellent times for meditation and divination. Open the space for what is deep within you to rise to the surface. If you don't already have one, try loading a meditation timer on your phone. Just five minutes of a peaceful mind can bring so much to the surface. Trust in the inherent depth and goodness of your mind; give it the chance to become knowable to you.

MY GENUINE SELF

I plant my feet firmly beneath me
And lift my eyes to the heavens
Seeking Your help.

Show me compassion through this day
Allow me to see Your divinity within myself.
Bless me with equanimity
That I may walk this day, and every day.
In my deepest truth
In my deepest love
As my genuine self.

YOUR NAME

The day break
Sings Your Name

The wind through the trees
Sings Your Name

The wave lapping the shore
Sings Your Name

The shifting of the Earth
Sings Your Name

The crackle of the flame
Sings Your Name

The night
Whispers Your Name

24

LAST QUARTER MOON

At the last quarter, the Moon is half-lit tonight. She rises around midnight and sets around noon. Look for Her this morning overhead and later in the western sky.

Just as the Moon—your deep subconscious—glows during the morning hours of the day, think about what is deep within you, what genuine part of yourself you can bring forth into the light. Some qualities in you may have remained dormant up until now, held back by low self-esteem or fear of failure. Now is the time to breathe deeply and dissolve the restraints that prevent you from fully developing your gifts.

Remember, you are not alone in this journey. A universe of beings surrounds you—each seeking their own happiness, each struggling to meet the challenges of life. Whether you choose it or not, when you let your true light shine, you are a beacon for others.

UNFURLED

Facing the light of dawn,
I spread my arms wide.

My branches are strong,
my leaves unfurled.

I am part of the grand cosmos,

My feet planted deep within the Earth, my head
reaching the heavens—

I unite above and below,

And bring life, love,
and beauty to this earthly plane.

SEED

Night falls

My day is done

Leaves have dropped,
branches have fallen.

I melt back to the Earth,
grateful for Her embrace.

Buried deep within

I feel the slightest quiver

Of a seed.

25

LATE LAST QUARTER MOON

Find the Moon this morning high in the eastern sky. You may have to search for Her in the sky; in the Southern Hemisphere, look for Her backwards "C", and in the Northern search for the "C" shape.

The Last Quarter Moon is a wonderful time to try some interesting divination techniques. Which method calls you? Pull a card? Swing a pendulum? Journal? Meditate? Maybe try something new, such as automatic writing. Or, make a list of the qualities of the deepest *you*, that you that doesn't often surface.

Do what calls you, welcoming these techniques as simply the keys to your own transcendent wisdom. They may let you see the patterns that govern your life, the ins and outs of your effort and resolve. They may point to the ultimate, mysterious goal of all of your endeavors.

SHE WHO IS

Let this prayer rise before You like incense,

Let my upstretched hands reach to You,

Let my voice be heard by You.

All praises to She
       who has birthed this land

All praises to She
       who nourishes all beings

All praises to She
       who lights our way

All praises to She
       who encircles us this day

All praises to She Who Is.

All praises to You, Goddess, all praises.

EVENING STAR

Beautiful Star of Evening

Guiding Light,
illumine my darkness

Tender Grace,
soothe my weary soul

Beacon of hope,
comfort me in my sorrow

Compassionate One,
bring me restful sleep.

Great Mystery,
I pause and behold Your face,
and surrender to the night.

Blessed Be.

26

EARLY WANING CRESCENT MOON

You can find the Moon low in the eastern sky this morning. She will soon be rising with the Sun; She is moving closer to Her Dark self.

Take advantage of the long dark night. Can you find a little spot of quiet? In a noisy active house, remember there is always a bathroom somewhere, and even a bathtub, that might bring a little respite. If you can, try and be up later in the night, after everyone has gone to bed. Sit outside in the night, and feel the calm settle in around you.

Bathe in the silence that comes when other voices have quieted, when noises cease to call upon your attention. Allow the rich, deep silence to awaken you to the spaciousness of your mind and heart.

LIGHT

What keeps me

    from reflecting Your light?

What shadows

    the glow in my heart?

What weighs me down

    and closes my heart?

What keeps me

    from authenticity?

Great Goddess, all-seeing and all-knowing,

Help me release what dims my light.

SURRENDER

What circles in my head and binds my heart?

What holds me back?

What am I resisting?

What keeps me from crossing to the arms of night?

Great Goddess, all seeing and all knowing
     Free me from my ties that bind me
     Free me from the sorrows and pain.

Great Goddess, all seeing and all knowing
     Help me surrender all that is not true
     Help me to surrender to You.

27

WANING CRESCENT MOON

Find Her early in the morning in the eastern sky. In the Northern Hemisphere, search for Her "C'" shape amongst the wispy clouds. In the Southern Hemisphere, search for Her backwards "C" shape. Around the equator, She will appear more as a "U."

She is preparing you for the Dark Moon. Find Her this morning, or seek out the tranquility of a moonless night. Make yourself ready for the deep plunge, the velvet darkness and infinite space that awaits you. Listen. What does She whisper to you?

TEMPLE OF STILLNESS

Great Goddess in the Temple of Stillness,

I find You in the tranquility of the dawn

I find You in the warmth
of the mother's feathers nesting her egg

I find You in the depths
of the winter cave of the bear

I find You in the waters of the deepest sea

I find You in the embers after the flame

I find You in the silence between drumbeats

I find You in the quiet at the end of the dance.

I find You in the moment between breaths.

Great Goddess, grant me the peace

To sit in your temple of stillness.

INTO THE LAND OF DREAMS

As I pass through the veil into the land of dreams

May I find You, Great Goddess

Lead me on this shadowy path

Across still waters

Into deeper darkness

Bringer of night

Shaper of dreams

I surrender to You

I open to Your wisdom, Great Goddess

I open to Your wisdom

28
WANING CRESCENT MOON

As the light decreases every day, find Her slim crescent low in the eastern sky in the morning.

You are approaching the end of this moon cycle. Throughout this journey, you have moved from the waxing full light to the waning introspective dark. Take a moment and consider where you began and where you are now. Give thanks for what time you have been able to devote to this.

Remember: very few of us have time to give our spiritual practice full attention. Please, honor what you have been able to do and value what it has brought to your life.

ANOTHER BLESSED MORNING

Another blessed morning to celebrate life.

The bee and the bison

The orchid and the ocean

The soil and the sequoia

The vastness and the variety

Today I celebrate the intricacy, the playfulness,
the chaos and the order of all Her creation.

Blessed be.

SYMPHONY OF THE NIGHT

The symphony of the night unfolds

The insects sing their hymns to You

The wind hums Your name.

The earth chants Your praises

You, Song of Creation,
know my innermost being

You know my thoughts,
my hopes, my prayers.

I too sing Your name

And release my soul into
Your symphony of the night.

29

LATE WANING CRESCENT MOON

This is the last moment until we fall into the arms of the Dark Moon. She is such a tiny sliver in the sky, you may not be able to see Her. Find Her low in the eastern sky in the early morning.

In the darkness of the night, find yourself held in Her deep and comforting embrace. Know that what you have found within yourself is precious and beautiful. You are only truly, genuinely *you* when each part is accepted, when each cell, each impulse, each thought is welcomed. This doesn't mean we don't work to improve ourselves, this doesn't mean we act on each idea—it just means that we accept these as part of our totality, our whole. Try spending a moment journaling about your journey and embrace yourself, in total and complete acceptance.

BREATHE

I breathe in
…and open to the Holy, the Whole

I breathe in
…astonished by the Mystery

I breathe in
…enchanted by the Unfathomable

I breathe in
…awed by the majesty of the Eternal

I breathe in
…sourced by the Unknowable

I breathe in
…blessed by Infinite Stillness

I breathe in
…I breathe out.

Day begins.

GRAND DESIGN

I open myself to the wondrousness of all

And listen to the messages
whispered by the leaves

And hear the words to the song
Sung by the bird on the branch nearby

And feel the pull of
my Mother the Earth below me,
hugging me close.

And I know that I am held, supported,
and part of the grand design

That my place in the cosmos is deserved.

Without me, the design changes

For no one can do my part.

END OF THE JOURNEY:
THE DARK MOON

You have arrived at the end of this moon cycle, a cycle filled with daily devotion, contemplation, and connection to the Divine—probably while living your usual life amid the work and joy and distraction of daily-ness, and the absurdity and busyness that pervades some portion of our time.

During this Dark Moon, take a moment to breathe and consider any changes that you have experienced over the last few weeks in your thinking, in your desires, in your experience of the texture of your days. What is different? What has risen to the top of your consciousness and called upon you to give attention? Are you able to be more aware of the Moon's circling around you, knowing that its actual physical presence accompanies you in your days and nights? Do you feel a stronger connection to the Divine?

A DAY OF THANKSGIVING

As you complete this Moon cycle, make space today to give thanks for the time you have devoted to connecting with the Divine.

Set time aside to reflect and journal about your experience, or perhaps schedule time for prayer, meditation, and silence. Go for a long walk and ponder what has changed in your life.

MORNING RITUAL

Honor your body with the following blessing. Take a moment to touch and bestow gratitude on all the parts of your body as you say this prayer, maybe anointing each part with an oil or water:

Bless my body that I may
serve and honor You in all I do.

Bless my eyes that I may see clearly.

Bless my mouth that I may
speak with honesty and truth.

Bless my ears that I may hear Your wisdom.

Bless my mind that I might know You.

Bless my hands that I may
work to create a sustainable, just world.

Bless my heart that I may be filled with love.

Bless my womb that I may
birth and nurture a grace-filled world.

Bless my legs that I may honor my own strength.

Bless my feet that I may walk always towards You.

Bless me O Goddess, I am Yours.

EVENING RITUAL

Take a few moments this evening in the Dark of the Moon. Breathe deeply, allow your mind to slow down, focus on the last 28 days and how you want to close this cycle. In the quiet of the dark, light a candle and say:

Holy Fire, Divine Flame
Thank You for the fire within me.
Thank You for Your Presence
Continue to lead me on Your path.

Stay focused on the candle flame for a few moments, and bow to the Divine Presence within that has risen to meet you during the last 29 days. Then close your eyes. Sit for a moment in thanksgiving.

Snuff the candle, knowing that the Flame of the Divine burns brightly within you.

CREATION OF THIS BOOK

We believe that people want a connection to the Divine Feminine and a way to connect that speaks the language of Great Mother. And, from our personal experience, we know that a daily practice is the bedrock of spiritual connection.

But, daily practice is sometimes a struggle. How do we find the time? What should we say? Many religions have a devotional prayer book to facilitate spiritual connection. This book is our effort to bring ease to the daily spiritual practice that can draw you closer to the Divine. And, by following the cycle of the Moon, this practice helps you become more intimate with the cosmic forces that shape your life.

For this devotional prayer book, we use the beautiful liturgical language and cadence of the past while recognizing and honoring the Divine Feminine. Some of the prayers in this book were inspired by other religions and spiritual systems, but all are rooted in our deep faith, love, and reverence for Goddess.

After the idea for this book took shape, we made a number of attempts to start it. We finally realized that we needed to be on sacred ground, in sacred space, for the prayers to come. We made a pilgrimage to the place we call a spiritual home, The Temple of Goddess Spirituality Dedicated to Sekhmet, in Nevada. The land opened to us, and the words flowed as naturally as flowers bloom.

Each night during our stay at the Temple, we gathered with other priestesses and read the names of people across the globe who sent us messages. We honored Sekhmet and all of the Goddesses in the Temple and of the land with ritual, song, and offerings of fire and flowers.

We hope we have captured the spirit of ritual, devotion, ecstasy, and love that we shared in that sacred space. To help support this sacred space, a portion of the proceeds of the sale of this book will be donated annually to the Temple.

MOON FACTS

We see the Moon all the time, but let's look a little deeper into some of the fun facts that tell us more about Her:

- The Moon orbits the Earth once every 27.322 days. This is the lunar cycle. In this guide, we track the lunar cycle from New Moon to New Moon. Compare this to the Sun's orbit (365.256 days), and it's easy to see how the Moon seems to be "zipping" around us.

- It takes the Moon approximately 27 days to rotate on its axis. This is called "synchronous rotation," and this is why the Moon doesn't appear to "spin" and why we see the same side of the Moon.

- The Moon rises about 50 minutes later each day.

- The side of the Moon we do not see is often called the "Dark Side of the Moon" (Pink Floyd anyone?). However, when the Moon is between the Earth and the Sun, during the New Moon, the far side of the Moon is fully lit in sunlight and the side facing the Earth is dark.

- Though there is no "dark" side of the Moon, there are some places on Her surface that are permanently dark, especially deep craters near the poles. Interestingly, these are the places where water may exist on Her surface.

- The Moon is about 4.6 billion years old.

- The Moon has no atmosphere or water and is composed mostly of rocky material. Craters on the surface have been formed from meteorite impacts.

- The Moon's orbit is elliptical, so sometimes it is closer to the Earth ("Super Moon") and sometimes farther away.

- It is thought that the Moon formed not long after Earth. Try looking up the "Big Splash" or "Theia Impact" theory to find out more. The Moon might be formed from debris left over from this impact.

- The gravitational forces between the Earth and the Moon generate two ocean high tides per day.

- While both the Moon and the Sun influence the ocean tides, the Moon plays the biggest role because it is so much closer to the Earth than the Sun. The tidal effect of the Moon on Earth is more than twice as strong as that of the Sun, even though the Sun's gravitational pull on Earth is around 178 times stronger than that of the Moon.

- The Moon does not generate its own light; moonlight is reflected sunlight.

- The Moon and Sun appear to be about the same size from our vantage point. This is why we have a solar eclipse. There is such a beautiful symmetry here! In reality, the Sun is 400 times larger than the Moon, but because the Sun is 400 times the distance from the Earth, they appear very close to the same size. It is synchronicities such as this that make the Earth a very special place!

- During the Full Moon, the Moon rises when the Sun sets, and it sets when the Sun rises. Every day after that, the Moon rises later, so that it moves from rising in the morning to rising in the evening. At the New Moon, the Sun and Moon rise and set together. After the New Moon, the Moon sets later every day, until eventually it rises when the Sun sets. And the cycle begins again!

ABOUT THE AUTHORS

Genevieve Chavez Mitchell is a student of Divine Mystery. She studied and practices naturopathy, homeopathy and herbal healing and has been active with the Women's Ordination Movement, advocating for women in priestly ministry. She has followed her own spiritual path which includes connecting with the Divine Feminine, celebrating ritual with family and community, and using her resources to create a more just, sustainable and life affirming world.

A priestess, photographer, a wife, mother and grandmother, Genevieve is a partner with the independent press Goddess Ink. She lives with her husband in Albuquerque, New Mexico.

Priestess, instructor, writer and dancer – Anne Key was Priestess of the Temple of Goddess Spirituality Dedicated to Sekhmet, located in Nevada, from 2004-2007. She lived intimately with each moon cycle, leading rituals and sleeping under Her light. In *Desert Priestess: A Memoir* she details her time at the temple and her journey to know Sekhmet. Anne is also co-editor of *The Heart of the Sun: An Anthology in Exaltation of Sekhmet*, a unique book which has both historical information and devotee's personal encounters with the Lady of Flame.

Co-founder of the independent press Goddess Ink, Dr. Key is the co-editor of *Stepping into Ourselves: An Anthology of Writings on Priestesses* and author of a second memoir, *Burlesque, Yoga, Sex and Love: Life under the Albuquerque Sun*. With Veronica Iglesias, she leads Sacred Tours of Mexico and co-created *The Jade Oracle: Deities and Symbols of Ancient Mexico*. Anne resides in Albuquerque with her husband, his two cats, and her snake.

SOURCES OF INSPIRATION

"Beauty" (morning prayer day 6) inspired by Navajo "Prayer of the Fourth Day of the Night Chant" found in *The Sacred Journey: Prayers and Songs of Native America* by Sargent and Streep, pg. 52.

"Goodnight Great Goddess" (evening prayer day 14) inspired by Zuni "Sunset Song" found in *The Sacred Journey: Prayers and Songs of Native America* by Sargent and Streep, pg. 35.

"Glorious" (morning prayer day 15) is inspired by "Morgenglanz der Ewigkeit," Christian Knorr Rosenroth, 1684. Tr. J. F Ohl, 1915.

"Let the Way Be Open" (morning prayer day 7) by Abigail Spinner McBride. Hear this sung by Abigail: https://store. cdbaby.com/cd/asmcbride2

"Radiant Heart" (morning prayer day 16) inspired by the "Golden Sequence" from the Mass for Pentecost, Veni Sancte Spiritus.

"This is My Mother's World" (morning prayer day 20) is a re-working of Maltbie Babcock, "This Is My Father's World," 1901.

"Today" (morning prayer day 22) is inspired by the Sanskrit invocation "Salutation of the Dawn."

GRACIOUS THANKS

Hail and great thanks to Sekhmet for Her guidance and constant support. Sa Sekhem Sahu. Gracious thanks to the Priestesses of the Temple of Goddess Spirituality Dedicated to Sekhmet and their support for our work. Special thanks to Genevieve Vaughan for the creation and support of the Temple, Candace Ross, who has carried on the legacy of Temple Priestess, and to Victoria Cattanach for welcoming us.

Deep thanks to Sandy Boucher, for her poetic editing and guidance, Rebekkah Dreskin for translating our vision onto paper, and Joanie Sather for writing our magical back cover copy.

Heart-felt thanks to all of those who read the first draft of this book. Your insightful comments have improved this work immeasurably: Amanda Thrasher, Maria Lotura Lawless, Samantha Sage, Vicky Moore, Cee Couch, Bee, Traci Leff, She of Many Names, Annie Finch, Cait Wallace, Trace Magaraci, Barbara Cigainero, and Abbi McBride.

We give thanks to Sophia, who continues to guide the way for Goddess Ink.

We would both like to thank our partners: Paul Mitchell and Ben Kuehn. Their love, support, guidance, and help make Goddess Ink possible. Your support is the wind beneath our wings.

OTHER BOOKS BY GODDESS INK

Heart of the Sun: An Anthology in Exaltation of Sekhmet
edited by Candace Kant and Anne Key

Desert Priestess: A Memoir
by Anne Key

Brigit: Sun of Womanhood
edited by Patricia Monaghan and Michael McDermott

Stepping into Ourselves:
An Anthology of Writings on Priestesses
edited by Anne Key and Candace Kant

Goddesses of the Americas:
Spirit Banners of the Divine Feminine
by Lydia Ruyle

Burlesque, Yoga, Sex and Love:
A Memoir of Life under the Albuquerque Sun
by Anne Key

Dancer for the Goddess
by Diana Rivers

Goddess Ink
explore a new path to the sacred
BOOKS ∾ CLASSES ∾ TOURS

All books available on our website or through online retailers.
www.goddess-ink.com